TOUCHSTONES

A journey through poems in xenophobic times

GORDON WALMSLEY

salmonpoetry

Published in 2007 by
Salmon Poetry,
Cliffs of Moher, County Clare, Ireland
Website: www.salmonpoetry.com
Email: info@salmonpoetry.com

ISBN 978-1-903392-69-0

Cover photography: T. Smith (with support from the Danish Arts Council)
Cover design & typesetting: Siobhán Hutson

Foreword

Touchstones was begun in Bretagne with a poem that seemed to come from a past still present in that place.

The book is written in various layers, in various patterns of movement.

Poetic sequences often move horizontally without titles. They are interspersed with vertical poems, towers, titled poems.

A figure, somewhat independent of the poems, emerges. He appears between the poems or between sections of poems.

This figure is the wielder of the poetic staff. He too, like the reader and the writer, is on his way to his island. He too has his story.

There is much in Touchstones that is of lyrical song. But there is much that mirrors the incarnation of something very cold that is decidedly non-lyrical.

In all this, the goal is to tell a kind of story. She who appears in the first poem and moves through others, has been with me in this. Along with the few touchstones I have at my disposal.

G.W.

Acknowledgments

The poem 'Twine' first appeared in *The Southern Review*.

Contents

Touchstone: A very smooth, fine-grained, black or dark-coloured variety of quartz or jasper (also called Basanite), used for testing the quality of gold and silver alloys by the colour of the streak produced by rubbing them upon it.

—Oxford English Dictionary

they came with their hands and the children
to sit by a sea to wait
stones lifting out of the waters
mists rolling over the bay

there there was truly a silence
and in silence a long-ribbed skiff
a figure in white she was standing
sparkling sea-pearled mist

stepping again to the pebbles
pebbles that hold in the sea
she brushed all gold from her seeing
breathing in wind that was free

I think of times of enchantment
stones above grasses in waves
and of how she would walk by a meadow
bearing the light of day

the old songs rise through my words now
and with them the numbers, the trees
the twelve and the five and the seven
nine and the four and three

yet this is a time of new moment
light comes in wisps from the sea
the children
running down pathways
to be irrevocably free

while she will pass through her gateways
hillocks cresting the sea
her hair ever lifting the sunlight
to spread over every tree

trees that lift in her heart's light
nearing the rumbling spray
in the time that is dark and golden
and we irrevocably free

first words

If life is at least one great thing
it may be it is a moving
through evenings and a morning
of tone-filled memory
in varying substances
subtle and also coarse
descending and ascending and descending
darkening and lightening
with blues and violet
and summery gold
and green that lays her hand
on a lake of mirrors
joined sometimes
or broken into shadows
dissolving sometimes
into crimson
then volving again
to blue that returns with us
englobing a world
smack in the middle
of all the other worlds
returning once more
our feet to the heavens
to what we call
Earth

Bring
what you can
to the silvery sea
in a silence most immense
with some few sounds
a stone's crunch
from the wren and the hobble duck
and a sun arcing down
into blood of a luminous island
rain on the water
pulls the gulls inland
and if you climb the hill to the west
you will find them resting on leeward slopes
so when it rains you are mostly alone
with the hobbling duck and the wren
you bring what you can
to a rage dissolved
to a whisper's sheen
whitening in silver
and what is above
is as it is below
the hermetic truth
split down the middle
and laid on its side
it still works, the old invocation
in the unseen world

and the world we now know
and whether you watch stilled memories
in a river s-ing south
or stand by a sea
where the gulls have flown
to rest on an unseen hill
you bring yourself naked
to the sea's reflecting
though this time
there are two young
doves
lifting away from the kelp
to the forest within
they seem to bless
the man who listens
across the darkness
in the echoing below
he is well within the silence of the sea
with some few sounds
he would know

Moving into the new time
we cherish what we have found
burying it within our breast
breathing over the threshold
we hope for the best
we think
this time is forever (the dark night coming)

we say
in the new time
we will sprinkle the earth
with thousands
and even if only one
sprouts
our lives will have been worth it

even if one child
walking along entranced
notices the one tree
its blossoms cresting in the May light
tucks it under his heart
like a letter from a secret friend
life will be able to continue on the earth

despite spiritual thievery, the depredation
of trees and things that grow
and liars in high places
who do what they can
that *their* will be done
hypnotizing us, either forcibly
or through the mild humming of electronic waves

they stand no chance
against even one seed sprouting
tended as it is by an old hand
or wind that sweeps the summer rain
no chance
and in the evening
a child with its head moving into the new time

releases a chute into a swirl of stars
jerks into a new night
where a tree with black crows appears
saying
you are on your way
you are really on your way
thank god for the earth and the loosening strands

and a dream that is no dream
but something arising from
a seed among thousands...if
only one should take...
that the night rain come
and sweep you into light
it is like a secret

buried beneath a limestone heart
found on a beach
on an island of ancient mysteries
a place of meetings
where the seed scatterers find one another
and disperse
then meet again

stirring again the fructifying waters
that the will of Love
be done
that beings bound to the inexorable will of the heavens
and the only beings who have a chance
of practicing freedom
(Man, Humankind, the Upright Ones)

may notice one another
beginning a new kind of dance
breathing across the threshold into a new kind of love
the times are
wondrously dark and light
and there are birds in a tree
luminous with orange light, they cast no shadows

on a thought clear as an angel's feet
you are on your way
you are well on your way
and if you are lucky
and work at it
you may even wake up
so those who would bend us

A Review Copy From

Dufour Editions, Inc.

Chester Springs, PA 19425-0007

Tel. (610) 458-5005, Fax. (610) 458-7103

info@dufoureditions.com

Touchstones

Gordon Walmsley

POETRY / American

Publication Date: Mar 09 2009

ISBN 978-1-903392-69-0

Paperback Original, 128 pages, $23.95

to their most finite wills
will be unable
to enchant us
with their dreams
of grasp and take
but will be
powerless

because of one small seed
someone noticed
when he was a child
that a tree might grow
its petals falling into the earth
that birds might once again fly towards the south
leaving the darkened branches behind

and leaves reddening in a fullness of light
falling, falling, falling
to form the golden circle

the round island

We arrive in our ship
at the temple of perfect freedom
to see the things
our questions have brought before us
we have built these walls ourselves
says one of the troupe
yet we have had help
says another
and nowhere in the world
can you find
such a one
as this

This is a place of perfect
freedom
where the thoughts that we shape
are allowed to be
seen
here, there is no compulsion
you yourself can choose
whether to press the coals into
diamonds
or to live alone with your lassitudes
letting worlds
go under

It is really up to you
and no one will tell you
what you must do
because in the temple of perfect freedom
each is his own king
and every king is a servant
and is balanced by the spirit of
discretion
and abounding
love

finding the island, he arrives at questioning
and the wielding of the staff

On an island of summer wheat
the rain is soft and fine
and what has been growing knows depths
few can imagine
it is as if the ancient goddess
were again teaching severity
the etheric mysteries of growth
and we her children
were wandering old ways
bearing the sun along
with our questions and resonances

Nothing is ever better or worse
than the way a man thinks
and the pourings of his soul
and the butterfly with indigo wings
is a surprise to us all
she carries a thought to a branch's tip
and when she is gone all that remains
is the thought, and a memory
of blues
and of shadows

I dreamt wisdom was a tiny
puppy, drenched with being born
and that it was peering shyly towards
great cities struck with fire
maddened prophets had tossed
on their way to heaving TETRAHEDRON
from sub-earthly chambers
and all to enchant us into obedience
in the name of global this or that
with religion, magic and please no questions
no questions

a thought running through tumbling times
when we see the deeds we have done
causing the fall of many a city
sleeping through schemes
we should have noticed
and longings for power
we should have observed
that which we thought was just plain crazy
has become possible
more than a child could imagine

People were meditating
in Colorado or even in Arizona
in valleys where scents
of don't bug me reverence
lulled them into easy enchantment
with dreams of peace and light-filled masters
whose water-tight chambers were nicely hidden
by all the right glows and heart-felt jolts
far far away
from the deeds of men

he contemplates the island

On an   island of summer rain
a rainbow stretched
over the hinterlands
the places behind
seldom noticed
receding ever into the background...
if there was a child running
heaving a sack of fish from the marsh lands
or ringing a bell of cool brass
it was because he was dragging along a question behind him

bringing it down from a branch with his bell—
the child who was running would sometimes pause
and in those moments he would learn listening…
dreaming himself into the old times, he would remember
moving legs, lowings and tinklings, the enormous
attentiveness of the flock
later he would awaken into the times we now live in
be fully awake in the light of day.
thus in these times of tumblings he came to understand
justice as compassion, not revenge, pulling himself together

he sought the untravelled roads
for it was there he would begin his life of meeting others
all in a summer in the hinterlands...
he remembered a prayer that was a kind of hymn:
our clothes fall away
we stand naked before the light
covered with silver dust
our feet glistening dew
the times we live in
can be times of mercy

for crimes
not yet committed
in days as yet
unraveled
in moments
before speech is brought forth
and breathing teaches
the circulation
of giving
and taking

the turning of the threads
is woven like a fabric
a tapestry
whose threads illumine,
dimming on down to a breath expanding
brightening then as we breathe on in—
the quality of the light we bring
touches threads
changing their colours, the wrongs we bear
move in colours of circulation, life and death

and the colours of our passing
trail behind in the waters of our being—
in days of young discoveries
we thought karma meant
boomerang justice—
people would say "bad karma"
or "that's karma" or "it's karmic"
and there it would end.
how could we know that what we called karma
is a vast sea of human intertwinings

it really is possible to penetrate, moving
as it does, through achings of human feelings
and though the wise often say
it is with feelings we must start
if we are to understand the interstices of men
it is hard to inscribe real pain
with the pen of consciousness—
yet in keeping the pain in mind
living into it
we keep a tension so answers may emerge

for what is a question if not
a tension?
thus said a voice to a child in the hinterlands
and then the voice said:
I am no expert and not much of a prophet
but I wield my staff
wherever the hell I like
pointing it into the strangest places
sometimes here
sometimes there

lifting veils

Start with an understanding of human freedom
and that all things have their time
and that to cling to old symbols
encourages error and possibly evil
as a resurrected sun-sign
becomes a stiffened menace
sun-sign darkening
to a demon
sun

Then with the possibility
of former inhabitants
moving on
as iridescent insects
finding a sun-bleached skull
move in:
the outer forms cannot be held

No doubt Averroës has moved on too
finding heaven in cyberspace
where electricity endows everything
with a semblance of spirit
while his old rival Aquinas
calmly proceeds with the work of
distinguishing the *qualities*
of the beings he knew
or sensed
behind the shifting veils—
that work could have been useful
to, say, Thomas Jefferson
who, putting aside his book of Burke,
walks across the candled room
to push a door
that turns revealing
delicious meats
"life , liberty and—not property, no—

the pursuit—" while to his left
the best red-robed humorist of all time, whispers
happiness
not wisdom or compassion
but pure unadulterated
Hollywood-style
Happiness
Jefferson was not to know
the source of his inspiration.
Unable to lift the veil
he would have to die through it
before he could see
that glowing being
who would have us fly, fly away
far from any task
of transforming spiritual lead
into spiritual gold.
He could have pointed
the land of the free
market forces,
as that whirling plenitude
of demonic beings is sometimes called,
towards something more
rooted
more sanely
compassionate
who knows?

II

I am told that angels
and all beings of the sun
and of all the unseen worlds
must answer
questions we urge on them

but that there is one condition:
that the questions be real.
Real questions must be forged
fired to just the right heat
plunged into rivers of ice.
Thus it is our questions must be forged
in fire and ice
because if a question
doesn't have
the right heat
no angel can hear it.
I believe that, say it many times
in many ways, and find it to be true
not because someone told me
but because I have tested it
letting it resonate
in chambers
consecrated to me
and you
long long ago
before the time when questions
could grow, as now
into sacraments
and when I think about this—
about the many-coloured marvel
of the question
think of it
as a glowing bridge
spanning our world
and a world of beings
possibly unseen
I remember
the beauty of a passage
of ION
who loved to lay his head
on the breast of Love itself

so that he could listen
to the spaces between heart-beats
and later remember
Pilate's desperate gropings to find
his way out of falsity, his world of Roman intrigue
to find...
and how Love was helping him all the while
getting him to ask
just the right question
and I remember the exquisite beauty
of the silence that followed

a silence saying:

dear sad entangled Pilate
Rome has bound you
with the threat of power
the power of threat
but I will love you into perfect freedom
nor will I disturb
that special tension
your question makes
as a stone in a pond
makes ripples
I will wait until
the last ring laps
ripples resounding
and when you ask me
what is truth
I will be silence
so that you may be free
and my answer
will be in no book

I guess
before all eyelids are raised
we are equally blind
and doubt if I could have seen
any better than Pilate
          still I guess it's permissible
in times of staged nightmares
to ask
          how do we forge questions
an angel might hear?

The Monologue of Colonel House's Inspirers, Servants of The Spirit of Ice

And Caesar Augustus
decided in a night
that in his world
everyone would be numbered
that the cold eye of governance
might easily fall upon them

Trying to do the right thing
we founded a nation
doomed to hypocrisy
and pedantry
where two things were celebrated:
the numbers we got
and longevity
everything else was bound to follow:
those who accumulated few numbers
were permitted few privileges
while those who had high numbers
were permitted more
thus we rewarded certain activities
while others
we ignored
those who furthered our apparatus
were given high-sounding names.
Those, for example, who were able to distract people
from our real purpose
we called "stars"
and we gave them very high numbers.
Those who helped create our giant
mechanism of control
we called geniuses.
They have perhaps the highest numbers.

It used to be
our numbers had equivalents
in paper and gold.
We called that money.
But there is no need for money
when it is numbers that count.
We convinced the gullible, the many,
that things were the opposite
of what was actually so.
They were made to believe
money had an intrinsic worth
and had nothing to do
with the assigning of numbers.
A clever deceit—
as though what they did (if it helped us)
deserved its proper reward.
And what was so ingenious
was we were able to suggest
(very convincingly)
that those activities we did not reward
were activities
that did not, may we use the word again,
deserve to be rewarded
when, in fact, it was often so
that the highest forms of inspiration
were the most dangerous to our purposes—
because they made people more conscious, or—
but more of that, later.
We rewarded only those things
consonant with our greater purpose
(listen to this it's brilliant!):
We spanned the world with a net
our cold intelligence could control
(the malicious would have it that it is we
who are controlled by cold intelligence itself)
and we made sure

laws could be enforced
anywhere on the globe.
We made the worst crime
disobedience to us
in all its varied forms,
compressing true freedom
into a tiny knot—
We remember a black magician's clever words, you
know,
the Englishman,
if you want to enslave someone
promise him freedom
and we lied oh how we lied.
And now we have almost realized our dream—
But excuse us, because we must now give way,
there is hardly any room at the top.
A top some say is actually vacant.
And we are afraid of rumors of love and of light,
things we do not understand,
cannot see:
Something about the light shining in the darkness—
never mind the rest.

Twine

In the world of broken hearts
we came to the river of understanding
wading out until we disappeared
we went down
glimpsing opening shells
and the rainbow of the sea
and the grasses never touched us
till we rose to walk the other side
by the river of earthly tasks

In the land of broken dreams
we did what we could
so people might learn tolerance
and not be crazy
because people were falling apart
their dreams no longer touching
the deepest part of a wound
in the land of scattered masks
when the waters were not friendly

In the city of broken nights
I vowed not to take my neighbour's shadow
for the real thing
but to leave it to its earthly task of
mirroring the gloom
my own dull slag creates
and I laid a prism on my heart
to change it to a rounding sun
or a standing figure
blessed with light
it would go right straight through to me
so I could remember
hold sacred
at least one thing
in the people you meet

In the house of sounds
walls were so thin
you could hear the neighbours whisper
voices flowed from room to room
bursting bubbles or lancing wounds
and we were filled with the noise of others
or a more mellifluous gift
a deeper kind of harmony
that comes when we
begin to discern
each of us bears a string of tones
we allow by grace to sound
and sounding along with the others
is like a marriage of all the brass bells
in every window of the house
and before the silent door
the place of rushing waters.

In the room of the shell
we lay the fragments
piece to piece
setting again the swirling conch
at the centre of the table
we set the cups
divide the bread
invite the neighbors in
and through the rainbow of the sea
we try to make out
the contours of a dream:
a ship full of prostitutes, thieves and shame-faced priests
is sailing to some northern place where the air should be
purer
each of us bearing the fragment of a shell
each fragment bearing an alphabet's letter
each letter bearing a sound in its womb

In the world of broken hearts
we came to the river of understanding
wading out until we disappeared
we went down
glimpsing opening shells
and the rainbow of the sea
and the grasses never touched us
till we rose to walk the other side
by the river of earthly tasks

No matter how bright
the sun may be
it will not manage
to obscure your light
you resting deep within
and I think I will be able to
feel your growing presence
the gentle piercing light-thorns
jabbing in the most subtle reminder
of absolute freedom's take it or leave it—
from a hub almost or maybe even that entirely
raying towards a periphery beyond the boundaries
of my skin, yet in touching just beyond,
meeting the other rays and weaving them both together
from another hub that is somehow strangely
exactly
the same self me
become you thus
me

Cross

Perspective
is part of a roundness
in seeing
as planets arcing
let a sun
grow warmth
into everything
or as sinking petals
in the jubilation of unfolding
release their life-bound blood
from lightest hands
ecstatic
dying
giving up the ghost
meaning spirit
meaning white cloud
meaning penetrating waters

Things are often other
than ever we imagine them
and "ecstatic"
is not what we imagined either
we never expected
a sunken head
nor the blues enshrouding it
we expected arms
crying out to an imperishable sun
never blue shadows
crossing the landscapes
or traveling among light-filled beings we dream as
distant

Their lives are much more near us
than ever we imagined:
since there are no empty spaces
to wield despair in us, but waters
limpid or turgid
with so much life in them
you would be astonished
if you knew

Understanding involves our own most moving inmost,
wandering pools of bright reflection
where heart, enamored of eye and mind,
embraces a path of its own inscribing,
becomes hands for marking, or feet
to step out spirals, whorls
or sea-coils
condensing then to pearls for stringing—
that she may sing more beautifully,
more truthfully.

We spend lives
dissolving the swirling shells
into openings
our hearts can widen
touching them
with the tips of fingers
releasing
          worlds

News Of A Day

Even truth casts shadows
and within those shadows
the broken shards of a mirror.
Strange images emerge
from the tired song of the newspaper
this seventh of may
a newspaper that is there
to tell you
what someone wants you to know
or not know
fragments perhaps to prepare you
for what might eerily unfold
dark enough to obscure your visions
bright enough to blind sleepy eyes

There is the desiccated face
of a churchman making a high claim
I represent All Christians. Past and Present.
And as for the future. I have laid
the strangest plans.
Through silvery waves of mirror
I discern the still living Christ
transmogrified into King Jesus, Tyrannosaurus Rex.
Thus Christ whose way is never

the way of command
is rendered as a tyrant
and the image of that tyrant
is the mascot
for the One True Church.
And the withered bishop of by-gone Rome
dangling a Pterodactyl from his neck

is seeking forgiveness
for the sins of all Christians
in previous incarnations
for the Cathars, the Templars, and Crusaders
the Most Holy Yore-Prone Church
was happy to burn.
I think of unsuspecting Charlemagne
who allowed a crown to be placed upon his head
without realizing he had inaugurated a tradition
thus falling into a redounding trap
so that if you wanted to be a real king
you had to be capped by a pope
that most crystallized caricature of Christ.

In another fragment
a promoter of cyber models says
You won't know the difference
between a woman of beauty
and our Helen of Troy. And guess what?
You won't even care.
It's the beast they ride that counts.
Apparently.
Another shard gleams forth India
who is saying
We love the Missile Shield.
India!
I think:
the pope, the Missile Shield, the cyber babes
have a lot in common.
No doubt the Missile Shield is a ruse
for ionic projections of King Jesus
as he arrives in a golden saucer
to touch a minaret in Damascus
or his virgin mother and wife, the harp-playing
simulacrum of the Madonna
riding her beast of prey, or even

the new saint Mother Theresa, feeding her billy-goats
in the shimmery stream of the Milky Way.
Cleopatra is also possible.
But of little use. And there is always Diana.
There may be more visions from
small children somewhere
who will tell us what we should do or expect.

Visions truly earthborn and bound for the ionosphere
though bound to the ground
and the tunnels beneath it, you can be sure.
A crazy idea in this time of total sanity.
Who could possibly imagine such a thing!
Only the lovers of small triangular heads
or of mantises
ever
preying.

he discovers one way the Spirit of Ice can
split the many-folded man into two

Inducing Trauma

Tunnels   caves   silent   waters

Tell them   now   if you   can

No one   knows   the depths   of angels

Or what   a thinking   *matrix*   can

a Hollywood film came by me a day
trying to split my soul in two
in so many films there are moments of
trauma
(and what will fill the empty room)
to pull you apart
from top to toe
(and what will fill the empty room?)

I guess that's the point in the twenty-first century:
to rip you apart so that something's shoved in
with tunnels and caves and silent wonders
blow you to bits
from three into two

A wise man wrote a book about freedom
in a faraway county over your hill
and in that book was a good suggestion
and this is it   hear if you will:

WATCH YOUR THINKING

literally   watch   your   thinking

inotherwords   watch thinking   as it   occurs

get it?   you should watch   the river   of thinking

is the idea new? (an american question)

is the idea, well, venerable (those who praise wisdom)

is the idea true (   )

well I think this:

truth being suspect in the twenty-first century

entire schools of french-fried thoughts

have been built to slur the search

they say:

a text is a text
with nothing behind it
do what you want
you free as a boid
or:
truth is a romantic notion
there is no truth but many truths
your truth my truth all in a circle
don't take your time what ever you do

yet a world eating cardboard
may decide it wants food!

all we want
is to figure out IS.
what's the story as slang used to say—
we just want the story—
Too much to ask?

You know the answer.
A mechanical voice intones it
loud and never clear:

we don't want you to ask questions
about what is the real story.
we want you to believe
no one can really know anything!
so go with the flow… go with our
flow

Looking   at thinking   I begin   to   think

what if   I look   at my feelings   too

say, while   I'm watching   this   Hollywood

movie   whataremyfeelings   whatdothey   do

(but you'll ruin the movie!

a small voice says (at least I noticed it)

(I let the small voice be

part of the world of what I observe)

and then what?
and then what?
and then what will happen
if I begin to wake up
and notice the tunnels, the caves and the splitting,
the plans that are laid for us
so we won't see
that in what we call the twenty-first century
the choices are mainly two:

(Hypnosis
or
Wakefulness)

or three

for in not choosing you choose to sleep
narcosis is the allure of the deep

Nonesuch Nonsense

in movings of sunsets
the meeting of hours
you lead me before you
mellifluous TAO
you whisper in gestures
too oft to be old
in running the horses
you dip in my skull
this was a morning
old 'nough to be new
so vast in its timeless
as good can be true
vast limitless timeless
swift waiting in sprint
your gift of a morning
lent love everything
lent love everything
our stumblings our own
through swevening hours
we listen to gold
when blue is a dying
and bells are green sails
and nights dim all lappings
we pass through gales
true you are the sun if the sun knows the sweep
weaving warm spaces
deus immolate
the mane of that maiden
sun-struck in a gasp
her heart taming horses
tethering our thoughts
she borrows a mane

(recumbent great paws)
and waters his trough
she lifts up her eyes
englobing the stars
she gives us our hearts
that we man learn "free"
in times of the wave
when sails can be green

he senses the sun within him

In the mind of a man writing upon a page
with a blue pen of plastic
in a room faint with the dew
I think of wildernesses and the joy of breathing
and what it means
to unfold a scroll of flowing silk
with words tumbling out of the south
following the ocean's warm stream
to this northern place
where a church of three towers
heaves itself out of darkness in the morning
and sinks back down in the evening's hush

so that stars and an invisible sea
may be seen again there
in a world of breathing
where that which will rise to exhalation
and that which recedes to the beginning
fashions between double seedlings
the soul's alchemical
tincture
a being of individual stamp
destined through warmth
to become something luminous
transmuter of self and the things it will touch

and that which is to be fashioned
is beyond man and woman
passes through many genders
in many times
begins as it does as a plant cut back
beyond memory and time, though allowed, in time, to grow
through recognition, nourishment and just plain love
out of the self's most intimate recess
a place deeply hidden
like a rocky ingress of the sea
where a path winds invisibly
through the place of mirrors

it grows within a spiraling plant
of two stems weaving
and its leaves and blossoms
are tinted with your own special
blood—and at the appointed time
you take them down to a river
burning with ice chocks
two stems that bear your own personal light
plunging it into that river
so the light can grow columnular with the heat
expand and be among breathings
to become your very I

thus the soul's sacred seed
becomes a sword, becomes a staff
fashioned among ice floes
in rivers steaming
with the thrust of iron
that we may make use of it
before the time of lifting
before we die
this is of course the great wish
to finish the things we have set out to do
at the same time sensing
remembering

as dew on a wall of a rose-coloured room
remembers in evaporating
how it has come to be
while we remember
dew is always a kind of blessing
that moves toward fulfillment
as a finger moves to send a string into music
or a mind moves toward waking
a morning of rising towers
when the early sounds of the wind's rustlings
in trees barely formed in an open window
allow for the most subtle realization

of a kiss drying my cheek—
it could only have been you
quiet woman of my dreams
you who lie beside me
appearing always
out of the blue
mixing silences in marvelous ways
too musical for us mortals to fully contain
you who breathe in ways I do not understand
so I can breathe a radiance within me
then out again into the greater circumference of beings
together with them you are fashioning
me

he senses the moon's dreaming ways and finds
again questioning as an antidote to enchantment

The time we now live in is a time of—
(let us not disturb the ritual of dreaming)

the time we weave is a time of dreaming
(let us not ritualize the emergence of wakefulness)

the time we have lived through
is the echoing of the time of averted glances

there, it is said.

and in the movement of turning away
a broad shadow sweeps along the earth

and within that broad sweeping
strange larvae spontaneously appear

they grow white in the moon's
dreaming ways

grow larger
and when the night stars speak to them

something takes place in them
so that in the morning the earth is as bright

as sun and clouds will allow it
and on fields and among trees

there are figures wrapped in threads
perhaps they are mummies of wakefulness

perhaps they are fruits of our dreams
we rub our eyes and hope for the best

but hope isn't enough when something new has been born
and our hearts have begun to stream as rivers will grow

when water pours into them, rain water
or waters of the sun, because the sun

is full of flowings if you become aware of them
flowerings too

what will be born in the time of averted faces?
will they foster growth in fields

or devastate our thoughts
will they move in colours from lilac to rose

or will they wrench doomsday from the earth
smashing it against the gentle raining stars?

the time we live in is a time of resoundings
of deeds reverberating in us

as we descend into earth-life, through the anguish
the terrible anguish of the past

there have been terrorful deeds on this earth
and there are many

hell-bent on being lulled into entrancement
lulled into turning the other way (though not the other cheek)

they do not want to know
Stalin and Hitler and Woodrow Wilson

not to mention Winston Churchill
holding aloft his famous sign of the Solar Demon (hidden)

were merely magically-laden vessels
of thinking's enthralled shadows

in times when it was as difficult
as now, not to be lulled…

that we were unable to help unseen beings
who need us to see, need us to hear

what they themselves cannot see or hear
unless we ourselves do—

beings in realms
eyes don't see

you can only ask
are we more awake than the somnambulates of other times

as we passively receive whatever is presented to us
on screens or sheets or subtle sendings, lulling us into

murderous deeds others carry out?
we live in a time of lullings

when the *heart* must learn to ask questions
and stick to them, must *practice*

the intensity of formulating within ourselves
questions

to be awake in the time of averted faces
means straining

for the question
that might invoke an echo, like

who gains when a nation's smashed to bits
then reassembled under a Logo–Most–Aloof

or how can a country intoning priestly virtues
choose Presipuppets who swear revenge and never

compassion?

to hold white moths
to the glowing earth

long enough to fill their wings
takes patience and not a little

love, so that when we have nurtured
the questions that are born in us

we can release white wings
to beings weaving stars

Permissible History

The official version of the century
has nothing to do with deception
or of the falling wave
nor of stones grown white
on a beach where two seas
meet

It speaks of two wars
some good side won
with the glittering magic
of freedom, democracy and just plain
greed

If there is a true story
it may tell of one war
visible or shadowed
now you see it
now you don't

This was a war to stamp
the heart of Europe
out of recognition
so powers of me-ness
might fully emerge
to strangle the world
in the name of freedom

To pull it off
demanded a plan
a very clever plan
with absolute obedience
and secrecy

The enterprise was to be
transnational as the slogan
Our World Order,
the *our* being mute
replaced by the word
new

The official version
says nothing of Christ's return
to the human heart
and of the obstacle course he would run
through institutionalised religiosity
and the various forms of electrical
hypnosis
meant to radiate the human heart
so that pure love might be replaced
in the name of democracy by
tyranny

I guess Freedom means the right to fall on your face
on the way to enlightenment
and to praise the falling wave
and white stones grown round
on a beach in Skagen Denmark—
and the right to recognize
enlightenment
is still
only partial vision

There need to be others
to round out
the picture
for every man is blind
in spots

In the official version of the last few centuries
Napoleon and Metternich were mortal enemies

and never brothers of darkling blood
and the trick of creating gigantic powers
by creating a semblance of adversity
was never to be exposed
Metternich was able to encourage an abhorrence of
France
to create Big States (easier to control)
trying to crush as best he could
the living spirit of man
wherever it could be found
creating a secret police
in the spirit of the Terror
or Pius The Tenth
much as Napoleon brought rationalism
clanging down upon the soft bosom of
Weimar and Jena
but the spirit of Steffens, Novalis and Goethe
was not to be undone
is not to be undone
for she who bears the light of day
shining Poesia, she of the many words of truth,
finds ways to fight cold thought
and foolish dreams of men

The official version of the century
has nothing to do with deception
or of the falling wave
nor of stones grown white
on a beach where two seas
meet

It speaks of two wars
some good side won
with the glittering magic
of freedom, democracy and just plain
greed, yet there is only one war
now you see it
now you don't

he tries to penetrate the mysteries of
questioning and finds Poesia once more,
she who moves within and without.
he reflects on his own country and sees people
dismantling illusions with their questions

Final Queries

In a world of mongers and passivists

how do you learn to form

questions a god might hear?

a man-child sits in electronic dream

before a blazing rectangle

filling his liquid shadow with lassitude

and dull excitement

he is far from the time he will learn to fish-out

just the right question

one that a god might hear.

he dimly discerns this world

of death and madness

where tumbling buildings can stricken a nation of

individuals

with the thinking of automatons-

is years, it seems, from the day when he will say

"I think *my* thoughts

not what others

would have me think"

and then

"*this* is what I must do.

my own thinking

has brought me to this threshold

and blesses the silence around me

not an outer silence

but the silence of
the brightening well
with the sun deep within it—"
in our world of dutiful drones
daily bathing in electric dreams
it is far safer to ask no questions
and the difficulty of actually formulating
just the right question
the one that would break open the whole show
is lulled into obedient stasis
don't ask, the dull voice says,
why do you want to ask?
what is called the news
clatters in with its shadow events
it's attempt to divert the struggling man
from the colossal effort
of lifting himself into waking
as a child's great and earth-breaking exertion
to rise from a crawl to a walk
to lift himself out of a daze
to ask
just the right question
is an act today
of heroic proportions—
to be a passive recipient of the official news
isn't enough today
we have to learn to ask questions

to hold fast to them over days, weeks
trembling seconds, months,
go out and poke around
that the gods might hear
questions resounding your soul
I suppose I am allowed to express such thoughts
in these days of intolerance
and guided thinking
knowing full well
there are those
who would compel us to think
in just this way, in just that way
thinking
involves clearing a space
and holding it open
so that what my soul can touch
what may arise within the folds of my being
a well
the sun deep within it
will gently influence even the most brittle of constructs
so the whole show can have a great fall
ask Parzifal, or even Perceval,
what it is
to forget

Freedom is a place between.
The surging glow of red waves
and the tempering tide that recedes.
It is a possibility
between before and after
between the gesture that urges
and the motion of restraint.
It is the absence of compulsion
as some of the ancients knew
and the moderns
were fond of repeating.
And it is one of the holiest words I know
and is especially loved by the
Christ

The Maiden is Young

That shining girl
knows nothing of blossomings
or of how the seasons run
why should she?
you have to be able to look back
to gauge the sweep of things
and it takes time
to build the right instrument, or a tower
that will let your eyes move across landscapes
time also to build a lighthouse
and always the danger
that by the time you finish you discover
they don't use lighthouses anymore
but a more subtle form
of drawing things near
a child in the midst of childing
has trouble with butterflies in the wind
wings fluttering
are not easily retained
by the mind's slow-growing fingers
whether the years will bring them back
is anyone's guess
even so
you walk across the room
through the slanting light
opening the door with one foot at the base
and a knee at the handle
stepping out into the rounding light
raising your hands up to everything
opening them
so that wings may find the wind

Double Plant

There are at least two blossomings
of America's dream
in these times of fake elections,
of plants and their shadows.

Ours is a plant of bruised shadows
drawing into itself vengeful thoughts
of purple intensity, with lava flowing from its roots
glowing red and darkening in its slow creep.

The deeds of a nation are sometimes like
deeds of a strange family of
dreamy fast-talkers, sloganizing
humanity's hard-won virtues.

Because ideals can be useful
to those who know not what they do,
greedily fondling
jewels of human thought for private purposes.

It is not wholly irrelevant
who wields the magic words
of freedom, democracy and
global religion.

For there are at least six darkenings
of America's dream
in these times of "the game". The game
of playing by the rules. Rules
foundering fathers
added to, long long ago

That the rabble, the people, might be kept in line
with no real chance of democracy
and that they might grow accustomed to
compliance, be more tractable, with blah blah
justice and little wisdom, for we are a nation of laws
and freedom for those we designate

as free, and don't you forget it
buster.
We will bluster the world with freedom
and amazing grace because we are a nation of lofty promulgators
like psychopaths pretending to be good

but who, when released on good behavior,
exact some horrible vengeance few expected:
rules and high dogma
and boy are we in trouble
because the glittering plant groans deeply
in the poisoned soil.

As for the other blossoming
it is the blossoming of the true dream
and that is harder to see
but I know it is there
watered as it is by streams
flowing from each of us
from secret places of the light

secret only because we have not yet
seen them
but they are there
flowing, refreshing, and building
the silent dream of America
a place where we get to learn
what freedom truly is

I think freedom has to do with recreating
your true intuitive self, and a land
that esteems this task
of fashioning
is the land for me, whether that land be
Denmark or America of Dreams
or even the Anointed One

come into earth to transform it
not judge it, to induce flowerings
and good sense, and even sanity
and careful respect, north of New Orleans
and south of Copenhagen, a land however
shadowed as any land is
by fruits of that land's most hideous deeds

Feathery Gold Falling

who would be a prophet

on the eve

of her smile

as a sun showers feathers

through the

blue room

it is something we dare not say

forbidden, as it cannot hold

either light

or that singing

and even if a subtle realization

brings us to an expression of well

thanks

let it be for small words circling

great ones

silence

keeps

holy

Towers

Surely somewhere
(what)
amid swirlings

of a cyclops' anguished limbs

a question must arise
(have)
from the marrow's deeper pain

so the eye within

illumines

words on the cusp of the soul

(I)

Surely something like shame

must tinge the face

white within its thrall

to rage
(done)
whose only love

is spawning

children of doom

that the conscience-laden question
(to engender)
be stifled

once and for all
(such)
murdering even

the rushing, thrusting, hell-bent

messenger

(hate?)

Touchstone

In the silence of a silver breeze
I decided to break open darkness
with a stone

it wasn't easy to come by
and had to be fashioned
from the blinking souls of

total strangers
their fears led me along a path
narrow and icy by a plunging cliff

I knew there was a sun
and that it was behind me
and peering all the way down

I tried to find my shadow
within the greater shadow
yet my shadow had merged

with the light
so I waited
for the moon

and its silvery wind

and when words came bright and dark
in a thousand shadings
there was nothing to be done

but to bear her upon my shoulders
up along the mountain ice trail
with sorrow spilling

from an ancient heart
and down across the windy fields below
my child I do not ask your forgiveness

cannot ask
your forgiveness

father, she said
I forgive your stupidity
but not your laziness

did you think it was I who
would be sacrificed and burned?
I am only the witness to your own

sufferings as it is you who must listen
and bear the pen
and when we reached the place of pain

I set her down beside me
and she began to whisper
and I took up my stone and smeared

gold streaks upon it
and I knew I was done for
because her words rang of truth

and I had to write them down
and small demons beat my arms
until my arms bled

and they tore into my belly
and clamped electrodes to me
to try to find out what I was up to

yet they had no inkling

because they were not of the light

I have been hard on you she said
when the thing had been written
I am glad you had your touchstone

to break open darkness
and I am sorry about the pain
but then, it was your choice

The Spirit of Ice

The Spirit of Ice
works through men
in many ways
goes by many names
his dilemma is
he is always
one step behind
the light shining in darkness
always past tense
looking over your shoulder
coming from behind
trying to enter in.

Electricity is his simulated blood
and his is the spirit of freezing
IS fear.
His catch-words are
zero tolerance
because his is not the spirit of compassion
zero degrees tolerance

He would like to implement a global justice
his being might permeate,
software-driven perhaps,
for who has created the icy templates if not he
we're tough he has his puppets say
we will use words in clever ways to
twist the Word on his cross of truth

His frustration is that he is doomed,
will pass like ice before the sun
and nothing he can do

can prevent Christ's flowing into this earth
he is, in a word, an anachronism
out of his time
behind the times
is the spirit of desperately holding on...status quo
and those who are desperate and fearful
know little of the patient growth of the soul
and they play into his hands
into the hands of the Spirit of Ice, of the
sad terrible freezing giant.

His ganglia are electronic wires
chips and worldly webs.
For he is behind your great technologic wonder
bent on creating mechanical justice and a
global economy
where great anonymous forces
reign.

His logic is the logic of sheer power, utterly
opportunistic.
Great world puppets of whatever disposition
are, well, dispensable.
He has priests too
to help him pull all power to a pyramidal top
to a spider's head, a head on legs,
creating many webs
that he himself might not vanish.
That he who is love
might not be heard
or even
noticed.

But human freedom
is not to be contained.
Because freedom is a flowing thing

is mild and infinitely subtle
and it's spirit is love which
in its form as a being
assumes the designation of the Christ
the anointed one, who is nameless and yet who
touches and loosens and works his
alchemy.

The spirit of ice would lull you to sleep
as a cold sea lulls men into drowning
and when you have your suspicions
say about global power
or Echelon
or the New World Order
(whose name is changed
to Global Union)
he would have you think
to dig any deeper
is too much trouble
his is the voice that says
why bother, everything will work out
just accept what my puppets say
my robot presidents and drooling priest
and then he says
I will bring you happiness
and where Christ says
I come not to bring peace but a sword

the Spirit of Ice says

he says he will bring a sword
but I will bring you peace

and where Christ says
my kingdom is not of this earth
the priests of the spirit of ice say

we want to bring the Kingdom of God
to this earth—
and so it goes, the way of ice
the way of tyranny—
but tyranny that would create a spiritual kingdom on
this earth
with everything you want
and one
lord
the Spirit of Ice.

Poesia

Poesia enters the silent room
she lifts her veil and folds it on the table
a sigh emerges from the threshold sea
for who has ever seen her face
there is a tumbler of water there
and shadows move over it like leaves in a window
we are at a place of absolute balance
before the hand touches
or the rush of swelling voices fills

Poetry is young and full of sad hope
with a heart that brims with what is not spoken
she raises her head from the stars below
and enters into their listening
then she melts into many pieces
to find the soul's secret coves
the harvesting glades of the mind
and within the eyes of those listening round her
not a word is spoken
yet when poetry draws once more into her own shape
they sigh like the rolling grains of the sea
for their hearts have found at last a sound

By the water on the table she places a silver cup
breathing her liquid thoughts into it
and those who are present sigh again
though this time
their sigh is like rain, like a summer shower
and not to be captured
and the chalice dissolves into a bowl
whose sides lift blue round the circle of men and women
and there is singing and singing and just plain singing
since a heart that is full can never be quite still
and must sing if it is to dance—

Leaving the room in twos and threes
in sevens and twelves
they try to remember like dazed apostles
what was said or spoken or sung
some remember words
and others phrases
and some remember certain resonances
and the colours
they bring

And when they awaken it is as though the colour
of the dawn
has tinged the waters of a glass bottle
poised on a table an afternoon
and they sense
the figure of a maiden
throwing seeds in a circle
and a sigh the colour of

shame

Birds are crackling

like burning wood

be brave

when the world is

tremulous

full of fire

they rise before the northern sun

a breath away

from a stone's

heat

Printed in the United Kingdom
by Lightning Source UK Ltd.
123722UK00001B/205/A